Praise for *How to Resurrect a Dead Prayer Life*

C. S. Lewis, when writing about his prayer life, once remarked, "The truth is, I haven't any language weak enough to depict the weakness of my spiritual life." Unfortunately, too often that describes my prayer life, and I suspect yours, too. Trust my friend and colleague Bill Thrasher to offer biblical and practical guidance, so we can resurrect our communication with our Father, who so longs to hear from us. Applying the principles of this terrific book will revitalize our prayers and our spiritual lives.

MICHAEL RYDELNIK
Vice President and Academic Dean and Professor of Jewish Studies and Bible, Moody Bible Institute; Host/Bible Teacher, *Moody Radio's Open Line with Dr. Michael Rydelnik*

With gentleness and compassion, Dr. Thrasher guides us into the presence of God, where our hearts awaken. He is a trusted friend whose passion for prayer jumps off the page. This book will be a balm to your soul.

CHRIS FABRY
Author and host of *Chris Fabry Live* on Moody Radio

This is not just another book on the importance of prayer. It is a book on how to cooperate with the Holy Spirit and make prayer a way of life. What could be more important for the Christian than sharing your life fully with the Father in prayer? This is a book to be experienced, not simply read. Whether you make the journey alone, or with a small group of fellow Christians, God can use this book to resurrect your prayer life.

GARY CHAPMAN
Author of *The 5 Love Languages*

No one will argue that prayer is not a key ~~~
ishing relationship with Christ. Yet fo
joy and power of this strategically im
elusive goal. We identify with the long
Jesus to teach them to pray. Thankfull

wonderfully stepped into that space to lead us back, or for some of us, for the first time, to an effective prayer life . . . reminding us that not only is prayer important for getting answers but also for the enjoyment of an intimate fellowship with Christ.

JOE STOWELL
Special Assistant to the President of Moody Bible Institute

Bill Thrasher has done it again! If your prayer life is dead, this book will blow life back into it. Inspiring, practical, and hope-giving, Bill's emphasis on the power of the Holy Spirit is spot-on and liberating. I've read this book twice, and it's impacted me greatly. Get a copy for yourself and a friend—it's life-changing.

KARL CLAUSON
Pastor of 180 Chicago Church, host of Moody Radio Chicago's *Karl and Crew*, and author of *The 7 Resolutions: Where Self-Help Ends and God's Power Begins*

There are two things I like about this book written by my colleague in ministry Bill Thrasher. First, I like how practical it is. This is not a book on prayer theory or even a deep dive into prayer theology. Rather it contains very practical steps and suggestions on how one can revitalize a waning prayer life. Second, this book is deeply rooted in Scripture. Yes, Thrasher shares personal thoughts and insights, but all are biblically rooted. These two aspects woven together make for a compelling and helpful primer on how believers can revive a stagnant prayer experience.

MARVIN J. NEWELL
Ambassador at Large, Missio Nexus

When Dr. Thrasher asked me to read his manuscript *How to Resurrect a Dead Prayer Life*, I wondered why he would pick me. He didn't, God did! I needed this! Highly recommend this book to help take your prayer life to a new level of expectancy and effectiveness, regardless of how good you think it currently is.

TODD HOPKINS
International bestselling author; Founder & Chief Visionary Officer of Office Pride

There are few people I know that embody a lifestyle of prayer more than Dr. Bill Thrasher. My life and ministry is the stronger because of his tireless prayers and friendship. This book, like his others, is honest, convicting, inspiring, deeply biblical, and intensely practical. Thank you, Bill, for never wavering in your commitment to model and teach the power of prayer. It has been infectious for so many of us my brother!

JOHN FUDER
Heart for the City; Chicagoland United in Prayer

I've had the the opportunity to experience prayer with Dr. Bill Thrasher for more than forty years; as a student at MBI in his classes, embarking on ministry, as our friendship deepened, and in recent days, as we both enter our "gun lap." In short, his prayers always help me believe God in prayer. So when this book landed on my desk, I didn't just read it, I prayed it! I commend him and this book to you; it comes from a man whose prayers have shown him how deeply he is known and loved by God. May the same be true for you, as you read it . . . but especially as you pray it.

PETER GRANT
Founder & President, PreVision Partnership

For years we had the privilege of sitting under Bill Thrasher's ministry. Classes were marked by his connection with the Lord, and through this, our hearts stirred to know God more. This book rings with life-giving accounts of people's friendships with their Maker. Careful reading of its hope-filled pages will enrich your prayer life.

HEATHER HOLDSWORTH
Author, missionary, conference speaker

How to

Resurrect

a Dead Prayer

Life

TRANSFORMING YOUR PRAYERS INTO A
SPIRIT-EMPOWERED, LIFE-GIVING ADVENTURE

Bill Thrasher

MOODY PUBLISHERS
CHICAGO

Scripture quotations taken from the (NASB®) New American Standard Bible®, Copyright © 1960, 1971, 1977, 1995, 2020 by The Lockman Foundation. Used by permission. All rights reserved. lockman.org

All emphasis in Scripture has been added.

This book includes excerpts from the author's book *A Journey to Victorious Praying: Finding Discipline and Delight in Your Prayer Life* (Moody Publishers).

Names and details of some stories have been changed to protect the privacy of individuals.

Edited by Amanda Cleary Eastep
Interior design: Ragont Design
Cover designer: Christopher Tobias
Cover image of gradient copyright © 2023 by jes2uphoto/Adobe Stock (186138760). All rights reserved.

Library of Congress Cataloging-in-Publication Data

Names: Thrasher, Bill, 1952-, author.
Title: How to resurrect a dead prayer life : transforming your prayers into
  a spirit-empowered, life-giving adventure / William D. Thrasher.
Description: Chicago : Moody Publishers, [2023] | Includes bibliographical
  references. | Summary: "What can we do if we're in a season of drought
  or have never experienced a rich life of prayer? This book shares
  applicable steps to prayer. Begin to breathe again as you offer your
  heart, desires, and disappointments to the God who loves to listen and
  respond to you"-- Provided by publisher.
Identifiers: LCCN 2023002400 (print) | LCCN 2023002401 (ebook) | ISBN
  9780802431554 | ISBN 9780802473219 (ebook)
Subjects: LCSH: Prayer--Christianity. | BISAC: RELIGION / Christian Living
  / Personal Growth | RELIGION / Christian Living / Prayer
Classification: LCC BV210.3 .T469 2023 (print) | LCC BV210.3 (ebook) |
  DDC 248.3/2--dc23/eng/20230331
LC record available at https://lccn.loc.gov/2023002400
LC ebook record available at https://lccn.loc.gov/2023002401

Originally delivered by fleets of horse-drawn wagons, the affordable paperbacks from D. L. Moody's publishing house resourced the church and served everyday people. Now, after more than 125 years of publishing and ministry, Moody Publishers' mission remains the same— even if our delivery systems have changed a bit. For more information on other books (and resources) created from a biblical perspective, go to www.moodypublishers.com or write to:

Moody Publishers
820 N. LaSalle Boulevard
Chicago, IL 60610

1 3 5 7 9 10 8 6 4 2

Printed in the United States of America

Dedicated to the Lord,
who delights in the prayers of His people (Proverbs 15:8).

To my wonderful praying wife, Penny,
who lovingly prays with me each day.

To my three sons and their precious families,
whom we view as a gift of God's grace to us.

And to my students and brothers and sisters
in the body of Christ who have listened to me
and lovingly interceded for me in prayer.

Contents

PART 3: EXPERIENCING THE GUIDANCE OF THE HOLY SPIRIT

PART 4: EXPERIENCING THE POWER OF THE HOLY SPIRIT

Forewords

I have known Dr. Bill Thrasher for over thirty years now. Each time I have heard him speak on the topic of prayer, he stirs my heart. I can tell I am listening to a man that is not only deeply rooted in the theology of prayer but is a man that also walks with God in prayer.

I remember sitting in his classroom and as he opened the lesson in prayer; his voice quivered with emotion as he spoke with God in an intimate and passionate way. The obligatory quick prayer to commence a class suddenly gave way to a sacred moment in the presence of God.

This is more than a "how to" book on prayer. The mechanics of prayer give way to the heart and rhythm of Spirit-led praying. The emphasis on the Holy Spirit's leading, filling and guiding our prayer life is at the core of Dr. Thrasher's message. May the resurrection power of Jesus move in such a way that your prayer life breathes fresh new life.

DR. MARK JOBE
President of Moody Bible Institute of Chicago; Senior Pastor,
New Life Community Church

My favorite classes as a student on the campus of Moody were taught by Dr. Bill Thrasher. I would walk out of each of his classes, sometimes with tears in my eyes, challenged and inspired to pursue this loving God more. I looked forward to every class I could take with Dr. Thrasher. I soon discovered the secret behind the power of his classes was his prayer life. I cannot think of anyone I would rather learn from on the topic of prayer than Bill Thrasher. I am convinced that your heart will be challenged and your spirit stirred as you read this book. I know God will use these pages to resurrect the dead prayer life of many people in the years to come.

DEE JOBE
Women's Ministry Director, New Life Community Church

Preface

It is my privilege to pray for the Lord's blessings on the readers of this book each day. Like never before, I am convinced that nothing is more important than crying out to God and asking Him to manifest His presence in our lives, families, churches, communities, governments, businesses, and schools. Please join me as God leads you also to pray.

Please do not look at your prayer life as merely a human activity. This book is about how God offers His powerful and gracious hand in motivating, guiding, and empowering you to pray. You will read how God transformed and resurrected my own (dead) prayer life. Even though I was frequently involved in the activity of prayer, I desperately needed our Lord to "teach me how to pray."

I pray that you will experience a revival in your own prayer life that will result in true life-changing prayer. May reading this book lead you to God-ordained fruitfulness in and through your life that will far surpass your greatest imaginations (Eph. 3:20–21).

Please know that I will continue to pray for you as you read this book, and I also humbly ask for your prayers over my life and family as God will lead you. I want you to join with me in praying for God's blessings.

Years ago, someone gave me a copy of several prayers written by Sylvia Gunter,[1] and I have followed her words by praying one of these blessings each day over my life, family, students, and the readers of my books. Will you join me?

Bless us spiritually

I pray spiritual blessing. Come, Holy Spirit, give our family a revelation of God as Abba, Father. Give us a love relationship with Jesus so strong that we cannot resist Him. Give us sensitivity to the Holy Spirit and hunger and thirst for righteousness that conforms our conscience to the Word of God. Create in us the fear of the Lord in relation to sin and genuine repentance. Give us holy joy in abiding in You.

Bless us emotionally

I pray emotional blessing. Come, give our family a revelation of Jesus as healer of emotions. Release healing to remove the ground for bondages (rejection, failure, resentment, jealousy, shame, etc.). Let us choose forgiveness for ourselves and others. Give us freedom from fear because God never fails us. Grant us a strong sense of hope to believe God for His promises.

Bless us mentally

I pray mental blessing. Come, Spirit of truth, and remove blinders of deception from our minds, so that we may know the truth and have godly wisdom and discernment.

Bless us personally

I pray personal blessing. Come, give us a sense of our personal value in Christ. Plant in us God-given vision for Your calling on our lives. Give us favor with God and with man.

Bless our relationships with authorities

I pray the blessing of right relationship with authority. Come, teach us submission to God-given authority and counsel. Direct us toward right loyalties, godly soul ties, and healthy friendships that encourage us in our walk with You.

Bless us physically

I pray physical blessing. Come, cover us with Your protective hedge of safety, strength, and good health. We plead Psalm 91.

Bless us financially

I pray financial blessing. Come, give us Your provision and right relationship to what You give. Let us acknowledge You as our Source and Provider.

With love, your brother in Christ,

Bill Thrasher

Introduction

I owe the idea of this book to the godly staff and leadership at Moody Publishers. They asked and encouraged me to write this book after I addressed the employees of Moody Publishers and Moody Radio one day. Since this is a book on prayer, I can think of no better way of introducing it than inviting us to collectively pray and believe God in the following ways.

> As You responded to Your disciples, when they requested that You teach them to pray (Luke 11:1), would You teach us to pray and show us when our prayer lives have died?

> Teach us all that You mean when You instruct us to pray in the Spirit (Eph. 6:18; Jude 1:20).

Lord, we believe You to lead us into the experience of being motivated by Christlike love and fervency as we pray.

Show us when we short-change our lives by treating You as our servant and not as our Master; and show us when we delight in the desires of our heart and do not find our greatest delight in You.

Allow us to experience the grace of prayer as we respond to Your command to seek humility (Zeph. 2:4) and guide us in repenting of any prideful resistance to your authority (James 4:6).

Show us when we are praying about the difficulties in our life and we find ourselves cooperating with the accuser of our brethren and not your Holy Spirit.

Guide us in accepting the prayer and ministry burdens that You also give us the grace to lovingly carry.

Show us how to use our temptations to lead us to experience a true delight in You and as an effective way to lovingly intercede for others.

Glorify Your name in the greatest possible way in our prayer lives.

Glorify Your name by restoring us to experience Your full blessing, and heal our lives and the lives of others who have been harmed by our sin.

Enable us to live in full obedience to 1 Peter 5:7 so that we can respond to Your leading in prayer.

Use our prayers to positively affect future generations.

Show us how to lean on the Spirit's help when, in our weakness, we do not know how to pray as we ought.

Strengthen us to believe You to finish well.

Part 1

FROM DEATH
TO LIFE

Chapter One

How to Know If Our Prayer Life Has Died

I was born in Montgomery, Alabama, and born again in the same city thirteen years later. Here is where and how it happened. Cramton Bowl is a football stadium that has hosted countless high school and college football games. While I attended many exciting football games in that stadium, none of them compared to the life-changing sermon I heard one evening there in 1965 from the late Billy Graham. He had canceled a vacation to Europe and set up an eight-day crusade at Montgomery's Cramton Bowl. Nearly a hundred thousand people attended, and an estimated four thousand people accepted Christ as their Savior. This anointed preacher and Christlike man preached with integrity, and God mercifully opened my eyes that June evening to understand the gospel. Before that evening, my desire for eternal life was only a wish, but that night it became a certainty and an understanding that it was a gift from a gracious God to one who could never earn it. This is when and how my life of prayer began.

Knowing Christ personally gave me a thirst to talk to God and read the Bible as I shared with Him my every concern. However, a lack of follow-up and discipleship led to my eventual stagnation of Christian growth. While I attempted to keep my life morally clean, I had no public witness for Christ and, at best, was a secret Christian. My life lacked any true intimacy with Christ. As I journeyed through junior high and high school and anticipated the future, I sought to plan my own life. I did not know God well enough to let Him guide and direct my ambitions. I joined the Air Force Reserve after high school, and my time on active duty awakened in me a thirst to cultivate my relationship with Christ that had begun at that gospel crusade.

As a student at Auburn University, I was experiencing God's blessing, but I knew that I was not living in a way that honored God. My life had the appearance of outward success, but inwardly I was full of fear, anxiety, and a longing for true peace. One day, I wandered into the room of a fraternity brother. He was unlike anyone else I had ever known. He had pledged this social fraternity on a secular campus for the purpose of leading others to Christ. As I entered his room on that cold December day, he pulled out a little booklet and started sharing about the wonderful discovery of the Spirit-filled life. I did not outwardly respond, but I hung on every word he said. The only thing I knew about the Holy Spirit was what I routinely and mechanically recited at church—"I believe in the Holy Ghost." That day I sensed the Holy Spirit was a person and the resource that I desperately needed.

Since both of our roommates were graduating, this dear brother, Robert "Buster" Holmes, and I agreed to be roommates for the next year. Buster had given me a short book to read on the Holy Spirit over the December break, and the illumination and understanding came during our rooming together the next year. God used Buster to draw me into Christian fellowship and ministries at Auburn. I had found new life at Cramton Bowl in 1965, but this encounter with Buster made me aware of my need to allow the Holy Spirit, who indwells every true believer (Rom. 8:9), to become a dominant influence in my life. This book aims to help you discover if, as a believer, you also may be grieving or quenching God's Spirit. You'll also discover how He can empower you to pray in ways you have never previously experienced. The Holy Spirit, who is called the "Spirit of life" (Rom. 8:2), can even resurrect a dead prayer life like He did my own.

As I observed Buster, I noticed that prayer was a natural and continuous part of his life. Therefore, I reached this conclusion: "Buster certainly knows more about the Christian life than I do, and he continuously lives his life in prayer. I guess that is what a Christian is supposed to do. Just as one eats and brushes their teeth each day, so a believer should pray."

As I completed my business degree at Auburn, I began to find joy and discovered God's power in prayer. My life was being blessed in numerous ways. I was being drawn not only to a full surrender to Christ but also to a call to a vocational ministry. I did not in any way feel like I qualified to be a minister, but shared with Buster how I thought God was guiding me. He responded, "God can use all kinds of people." That word filled my life with hope.

When I felt the need to close the door to some good job opportunities in business, I explored pursuing an MBA at Harvard University. At that time, two Harvard

MBA graduates were on staff with Campus Crusade for Christ, now Cru. I would go to the Auburn University library and look at the Harvard catalog, but never had any peace about this direction. I now know more clearly that administration is not at all my primary gift. What I really wanted to do was work in a college ministry and help others experience Christ in the way that I had been helped at Auburn. The counsel of my parents and other older and wiser believers encouraged me to get training. I resisted this advice because to me it seemed like the more a person knew about the Christian faith, the less excited they were about it. Why would I want what they had? However, I desperately needed training and I eventually accepted this wise counsel.

After graduating from Auburn, I did a summer pastoral internship in Chattanooga, Tennessee, under Ben Haden. He had been saved as an adult and worked as a lawyer, newspaper executive, and with the CIA before serving as a pastor. That summer, he treated me like a son and gave much needed counsel as I prepared to attend seminary in the fall.

My seminary experience was a four-year, 120-hour program leading to a master's in theology. I studied with a true desire to learn that I had never previously experienced.

In the process of this training, I sensed a leading to go into teaching, to which I was quite resistant. The common stereotype of my fellow seminarians was that the warm- and tender-hearted ones wanted to be pastors and missionaries, and the more cerebral types desired to be professors. I felt an affinity with the former group, but God overcame my reluctance, just as He had my initial resistance to go to seminary. My professors encouraged me to apply for a doctoral program, which I did, and this resulted in two more years of training.

After these six years of intense seminary study, God graciously provided an invitation to go to Chicago to interview for a teaching position at the Moody Bible Institute. The Lord in His kindness opened this door, and this is where I have served for well over forty years.

In this pilgrimage—rooming with Buster at Auburn, doing several pastoral internships, and all my years of academic study—I sought to live a life of prayer each day. I had prayer meetings in my seminary dorm room each night and would meet with others for extended nights of prayers on the weekends. I sought to continue this discipline of prayer as I began my teaching ministry at Moody—until one day . . .

This day when I was diligently pursuing my discipline of prayer, I discovered that something had happened. I also found myself entertaining this very loud thought: "Lord, one of the greatest gifts You could give me is to take this burden of prayer off my back." Why had it become such a burden? Because in the ten years since discovering the filling of the Spirit and the joy of prayer, I had been met with many exhortations to pray. I had discovered many things that others said were important to pray for, and I diligently sought to do so. However, on this day, I discovered that my prayer life had died even though I was very involved in the activity of prayer.

How do you know if your prayer life has died? It is when you are praying and yet are not expecting anything to happen. That is where I was. And that is why I found myself asking God to take this burden of prayer off my back.

If you had asked me to summarize the teaching of prayer that I continually heard, it would be these two things:

1. Prayer is very, very important.
2. You need to discipline yourself to do it.

These are two essential foundational truths that one must embrace for any additional prayer insight not to be

29

only theoretical. However, I had fully embraced these two truths and even built my life around them, but my prayer life had died.

The good news is that there is life after death. You can believe God to restore and resurrect your prayer life. Believe God for this as you keep reading, and even trust Him to use you to lead many others to experience a transformation from mere involvement in the activity of prayer to a Spirit-empowered and life-giving discipline.

For Personal or Group Reflection

Describe how your Christian life began.

How do you know if your prayer life has died?

Chapter Two

How to Develop Fervency and Compassion in Our Prayer Life

D. L. Moody, considered by most of his contemporaries as the greatest preacher of his day, said that he would rather teach one person to pray than ten people to preach. I certainly knew that I needed to be taught by God something more than that prayer was important and I needed to discipline myself to do it. I saw in the Scripture that when the Lord's disciples cried out to Him and said, "Lord, teach us to pray," that He responded (Luke 11:1). Just as He responded to His first-century disciples, He is eager to respond to us today as we ask Him to teach us to pray! Jesus informed His disciples that He would send the Spirit to be with them and help them in any way they needed divine support. Five commands in Scripture are directly connected to the Holy Spirit:

1. Walk by the Spirit (Gal. 5:16)
2. Be filled with Spirit (Eph. 5:18)
3. Don't grieve the Spirit (Eph. 4:30)
4. Don't quench the Spirit (1 Thess. 5:19)
5. Pray in the Spirit (Eph. 6:18; Jude 1:20)

This fifth command got my attention in a special way. It teaches us that meaningful prayer is not something that God expects any of us to sustain by ourselves. We need divine help, and that is exactly what Jesus promised to send to His disciples (John 14:16). The Holy Spirit is called a "Paraclete" or "One called alongside to help." This help is always available because He is promised to be with us forever and even to indwell us (John 14:16–17). Every true believer can count on Him to guide them into truth and enable them to glorify Christ (John 16:13–14).

The starting place to receive God's help is to admit your need for it. Look at the many promises God gives to those who admit all their needs. Here are just a few of them:

1. Promises to the needy as we navigate family life

   Psalm 72:4–5: "Save the children of the needy." (I always felt my children qualified for this!)

   Psalm 107:41–42: "But He sets the needy securely on high, away from affliction, and makes his families like a flock. The upright see it and are glad; but all injustice shuts its mouth."

2. Promises to the needy as we seek guidance

   Jeremiah 10:23: "I know, LORD, that a person's way is not in himself, nor is it in a person who walks to direct his steps."

3. Promises to the needy as we seek wisdom

   Romans 1:22: "Claiming to be wise, they became fools."

   1 Corinthians 3:18: "Take care that no one deceives himself. If anyone among you thinks that he is wise in this age, he must become foolish, so that he may become wise."

James 1:5: "But if any of you lacks wisdom, let him ask of God, who gives to all generously and without reproach, and it will be given to him."

4. Promises to the needy as we seek to receive God's gracious enablement

James 4:6: "But He gives a greater grace. Therefore, it says, 'God is opposed to the proud, but gives grace to the humble.'"

It was not hard for me to admit my desperate need of divine help regarding my prayer life. For that reason, I began the journey of asking God to show me what it meant to pray in the Spirit.

One of the first things I learned was that I needed divine help to motivate my prayer life. I discovered that we must first confess the following truth, as unflattering as it is: "Lord, I confess that in and of myself, I do not really care about anybody but myself." Apart from Jesus' liberating work of the cross and the enablement of the Spirit, the only life anyone of us could ever know is one filled with selfish ambition and motivated by "what is in it for me?" We are not able to pray with Christlike fervency and Christlike compassion without His divine help.

As we read Scripture, we observe God's loving rebuke to the one who does not "[stir himself to take hold of God]" (Isa. 64:7) and to those who only "[honor the Lord] with their lips, but their heart is far away from [Him]" (Matt. 15:8). How does this apply to praying believers? Jesus would rather the prayers of our hearts be without words than our words without heart. Jesus' loving correction and empowerment can enable the believer to not be judgmental but rather shed tears of compassion for those who disobey God (Ps. 119:36) and pray with a fervent heart (Acts 12:5). How do we depend upon the Holy Spirit to develop this Christlike compassion and fervency in our prayer life? How can we be delivered from being involved in much praying where there is no true prayer? How can we be delivered from praying and not really meaning anything as we pray?

- The first step is to open your life up to the Spirit and let Him enable you to realize a real need for which to pray.
- The second step is to live with what you have been shown so that you begin to feel this need in a way that your heart is truly gripped by it.

- The next step is to realize and admit your helplessness to do anything about it. We cannot ultimately change our own life, much less the lives of others.
- These will lead you to the final step of surrendering the whole matter to God and crying out with the compassionate and fervent cry that the Spirit of God is developing in you if you get out of the way.

It's a delusion to think that we cannot pray, because we can if we truly want something. It is not our eloquence or beautiful language that God responds to. But it is the cry that comes from the heart in which the Spirit of God has truly placed a compassionate prayer burden. To this cry, God delights to hear and respond.

Join me in this journey of trusting the Lord to "teach you to pray," and remember that Jesus will respond to this request (see Luke 11:1). Know that He invites us to learn from Him and that He is a gentle teacher (Matt. 11:29). True prayer delights the heart of God (Prov. 15:8). I have so appreciated how God has even helped me unlearn things about prayer that were wrong, as you will see as you read this book. He is a living God who is infinite and can listen to your concerns and questions as if you were the only person talking to Him; this will not take His attention away from anyone else! The key is to be childlike enough to believe that if God gives you a command, you can trust Him to explain it to you in ways that you can understand it and to enable you to experience it in your life. If He commands something, we know it is His will. If we know it is His will, we can be assured that He will both hear and answer our prayer (1 John 5:14–15). You can be sure that as you keep reading and keep trusting God to understand and obey His command, He will answer you in His timing and way.

Why not trust God for a companion to join you in this journey? This companion may be a spouse, a child, or a close friend, or even a group of people. I will be joining you in prayer that God will lead all the readers of this book, along with me, into a deeper understanding of God's divine help in our prayer lives as we journey together.

For Personal and Group Reflection

Look at the five commands that are given in relationship to the Holy Spirit and pray in faith to be led into the experience of each one.

Pray over the four bullet points in developing Christlike compassion and fervency in your prayer life, and note any insights that God gives you.

Part 2

EXPERIENCING THE MOTIVATION OF THE HOLY SPIRIT

Chapter Three

Halting Our Fleshly Scheming and Embracing God's Authority

The testimony of a believing wife who was praying for her husband's salvation is one that I will never forget. She knew the Scripture that instructed her not to preach at him or nag him (1 Peter 3:1–2). So, she secretly schemed and placed numerous books throughout the house that were opened to the exact pages she desired her husband to read. However, God convicted her of these actions. "Only after I responded to God's convicting me of my fleshly scheming did my husband come to faith," she stated. It seemed that God had used her own trustful surrender to the Lord to prompt her husband's trust and surrender to the

Lord. Before, it must have appeared to her husband that she was asking him to trust in her God for his eternal salvation, but she was not viewing her God as capable of caring for her concern. We can easily fall into the same tendencies in our prayer life.

Many of us remember where we were when we learned of the events of September 11, 2001. Three hijacked passenger planes carried out coordinated suicide attacks against the World Trade Center in New York City and the Pentagon in Washington DC, killing everyone on board the planes and nearly three thousand people on the ground. A fourth plane crashed in a Pennsylvania field, killing all on board after a courageous effort by the passengers and crew to wrestle control away from the hijackers. I was teaching a seminary class on the sovereignty and the mercy of God when someone from the administration entered the classroom and quietly informed me of the event and alerted me that the school officials were considering ordering an evacuation of the campus. Shortly afterward, we received instructions to leave the campus.

That afternoon, I walked through Chicago on my way to the station to catch a train to the suburbs—the city was a ghost town. Once home, and feeling many emotions,

I sought to gather my wife and my three young sons to pray. As I contemplated this senseless and cruel taking of human life, God brought to my mind the words of Jesus in Matthew 5:21 and 22, which states that if we have been angry with our brother, we, too, are guilty of murder. I felt led by God to begin our family prayer meeting by confessing to my family that I, too, was a murderer. That was a necessary preparation to pray for the murderers of September 11.

As we pray to the Lord, we need to always be open to these two questions:

1. Are we willing to adjust our lives in any way that God will direct us to?
2. Are we willing to involve our lives in the answers to our prayers?

How we respond to God's loving correction as we pray reveals a lot about our character (Prov. 9:8–9). A revival happened many years ago at a Christian high school that my sons later attended. It was started by a group of mothers who gathered to pray for their sons and daughters. As they prayed, God convicted them of things that they needed to confess to their children. That is what sparked the revival—their convictions primed the pump from which God's blessings flowed. This is not a mechanical formula, but rather an example of embracing the truth that we can't be praying for others and ignoring what God wants to be adjusting in our lives.

We are told that dreaming can be a healthy part of sleeping and that everyone dreams several times a night. Although I seldom remember my dreams, I will relate one that I do remember. The only detail I recall was walking along a street with a stranger who had spoken very inappropriately to a young lady who had crossed our paths. I turned to him in great concern and asked, "What did you say?" The dream then fast-forwarded to a church service that was about to begin. At the service, the stranger in my dream was seated by himself in deep remorse and repentance. As his family approached to join him, his son came up to him and began confessing his own sin to his father and asking for forgiveness. At that point, I awakened from my sleep and wrote down this dream in excitement. This dream is a picture of revival. The repentant father had reached the son, even though the son knew nothing of his father's actions. The son simply felt free to approach his father to confess his own sins.

After James wrote, "You do not have, because you do not ask," he evidently anticipated an objection from his readers, arguing that they were asking continually and were still not receiving. To this anticipated objection, James replied that the reason for their asking and not receiving was that "you ask with the wrong motives, so that you may spend what you request on your pleasures" (James 4:2–3). This certainly does not mean that we cannot pray for our desires, but it does mean that our desires are not to be the lord of our lives. When we pray in this way, we are treating God as our servant and not as our Master. The solution to which James leads us to is to submit ourselves to God. When we are under His authority, we can experience spiritual authority over the devil (James 4:7). Under God's authority you and I are also free to express our desires to God as our Lord did in Gethsemane when He asked the Father to "remove this cup from Me." He also submitted His desire to the Father by praying, "Yet not what I will, but what You will" (Mark 14:36).

When the wife at the beginning of this chapter ceased from her scheming and surrendered to God her desires for her husband's salvation, things began to change; but the first change was in her. When those mothers confessed their own sins to their children, what they desired to happen was set in motion above and beyond anything they could have imagined. Like the father in the dream who responded to God's conviction, we, too, can be restored and also lead others to repentance.

Our responsibility is clear—to delight ourselves in the Lord, to commit our way to Him, and to trust Him and watch Him work (Ps. 37:4–5). When we repent of our scheming and our idolatrous desires, He will show us our part. If we delight ourselves in the desires of our heart, we will experience needless conflicts with all who get in the way of our goals, and we will never experience true fulfillment (see James 4:1–2). The path of delighting in the Lord is the only one that enables God to both transform us and give us the true desires of our hearts.[1] The next chapter will seek to aid in your experience of this in your life.

For Personal and Group Reflection

Ask God to show you how you might be treating Him as your servant and not your master, and note any insight that God gives you.

Chapter Four

Learning to Seek Humility

God is opposed to the proud but gives grace to the humble, according to James 4:6. God's grace in the Christian life includes the provision of the Spirit to motivate and enable the believer to obey God. This grace is the key to all our efforts. This book is designed to aid you in experiencing this grace in your prayer life. It is therefore fitting to look at how to grow in this grace, which we are actually commanded to do (2 Peter 3:18).

The little book of Zephaniah may not be the most well known in Scripture, but it is full of helpful truths. One of these truths is the gracious command to "seek humility" (Zeph. 2:3). God enables us to grow in grace as we grow in humility. This command to seek humility, as strange as it may sound, caught my attention in a special way. Scripture meditation combines the discipline of Scripture with the discipline of prayer as Jesus instructs us to do in John 15:7. It is simply talking to God about His Word with a desire that your life would come into an agreement with it. It is a discipline that God promises to bless (Josh. 1:8–9; Ps. 1:1–3). As I asked God to explain this command in Zephaniah to me, these are the conclusions I came to. I pray that each of these will aid you in experiencing the grace of prayer. Let me encourage you to simply pray through the Scriptures under each heading. This is the meditation that God promises to bless!

Seeking Humility Means Not Trying to Be God

1. God alone is our ultimate authority:

> So David blessed the LORD in the sight of all the assembly; and David said, "Blessed are You, LORD God of Israel our father, forever and ever. Yours, LORD, is the greatness, the power, the glory, the victory, and the majesty, indeed everything that is in the heavens and on the earth; Yours is the dominion, LORD, and You exalt Yourself as head over all." (1 Chron. 29:10–11)

"But at the end of that period, I, Nebuchadnez-
zar, raised my eyes toward heaven and my reason
returned to me, and I blessed the Most High and
praised and honored Him who lives forever;

> For His dominion is an everlasting dominion,
> And His kingdom endures from generation
> to generation.
> All the inhabitants of the earth are of no
> account,
> But He does according to His will among the
> army of heaven
> And among the inhabitants of earth;
> And no one can fend off His hand
> Or say to Him, 'What have You done?'"
> (Dan. 4:34–35)

We seek humility by submitting to His authority as
we pray. This is the pathway to experience not only spiritual authority (James 4:7), but also correct thinking, "My
reason returned to me" (Dan. 4:36).

2. God alone is the ultimate lawgiver and judge:

> Do not speak against one another, brothers and sisters. The one who speaks against a brother or sister, or judges his brother or sister, speaks against the law and judges the law; but if you judge the law, you are not a doer of the law but a judge of it. There is only one Lawgiver and Judge, the One who is able to save and to destroy; but who are you, judging your neighbor? (James 4:11–12)

We seek humility by refraining to set ourselves up as anyone's ultimate judge and by not engaging in any of the following practices that would greatly hinder our prayer life:

- Gossip—sharing detrimental information with those who are not part of the problem or solution
- Slander—telling the truth with the desire to hurt
- Anything that violates God's commands to "honor all people" (1 Peter 2:17)

3. God alone knows and controls the future:

Come now, you who say, "Today or tomorrow we will go to such and such a city, and spend a year there and engage in business and make a profit." Yet you do not know what your life will be like tomorrow. For you are just a vapor that appears for a little while, and then vanishes away. Instead, you ought to say, "If the Lord wills, we will live and also do this or that." But as it is, you boast in your arrogance; all such boasting is evil. (James 4:13–16)

We seek humility by trusting God to guide us in our planning and even in submitting the plans He has given us to Him as we pray.

4. God alone is the source of all blessing:

Every good thing given and every perfect gift is from above, coming down from the Father of lights, with whom there is no variation or shifting shadow. (James 1:17)

We seek humility by realizing, as we pray, that everything we are and have is the gift of a gracious God.

For who considers you as superior? What do you have that you did not receive? And if you did receive it, why do you boast as if you had not received it? (1 Cor. 4:7)

But by the grace of God I am what I am, and His grace toward me did not prove vain; but I labored even more than all of them, yet not I, but the grace of God with me. (1 Cor. 15:10)

Both riches and honor come from You, and You rule over all, and in Your hand is power and might; and it lies in Your hand to make great and to strengthen everyone. Now therefore, our God, we thank You, and praise Your glorious name. "But who am I and who are my people that we should be able to offer as generously as this? For all things come from You, and from Your hand we have given to You." (1 Chron. 29:12–14)

We also seek humility by repenting when we lose sight of this truth.

Now as for me, I said in my prosperity,
"I will never be moved."
LORD, by Your favor You have made my mountain to
stand strong;
You hid Your face, I was dismayed. (Ps. 30:6–7)

Seeking Humility Means Admitting Our Need

Christ's most serious rebuke was given to the church of Laodicea, which didn't recognize its need but instead became blinded by its abundance. He quotes them to clearly communicate that it is their self-sufficiency that evokes this response: "So because you are lukewarm, and neither hot nor cold, I will vomit you out of My mouth. Because you say, 'I am rich, and have become wealthy, and I have need of nothing,' and you do not know that you are wretched, miserable, poor, blind, and naked" (Rev. 3:16–17).

We seek humility by confessing our sins that God points out in our lives.

If we confess our sins, He is faithful and righteous to forgive us our sins and to cleanse us from all unrighteousness. If we say that we have not sinned, we

make Him a liar and His word is not in us.
(1 John 1:9–10)

We seek humility by admitting our fear and anxieties and bringing them to God in prayer.

Therefore humble yourselves under the mighty hand of God, that He may exalt you at the proper time, having cast all your anxiety on Him, because He cares about you. (1 Peter 5:6–7)

I sought the Lord and He answered me,
And rescued me from all my fears. (Ps. 34:4)

We seek humility by acknowledging our anger and letting Christ heal our hurts as we lay them before Him in prayer.

Be angry, and yet do not sin; do not let the sun go down on your anger, and do not give the devil an opportunity. (Eph. 4:26–27)

We seek humility by acknowledging our inability to guide our own life and looking to Him in prayer for guidance.

I know, LORD, that a man's way is not in himself,
Nor is it in a man who walks to direct his steps.
(Jer. 10:23)

We seek humility by admitting our need for God's enablement and choosing to trust Him in prayer for all our responsibilities.

"I am the vine, you are the branches; the one who remains in Me, and I in him bears much fruit, for apart from Me you can do nothing." (John 15:5)

We seek humility by admitting our need for God's provisions and praising Him as our Jehovah Jireh (the Lord Who Provides).

And my God will supply all your needs according to His riches in glory in Christ Jesus. (Phil. 4:19)

We seek humility by admitting our need for God as our protector as we express our trust of Him in prayer.

The LORD is my strength and my shield;
My heart trusts in Him, and I am helped;
Therefore my heart exults,
And with my song I shall thank Him. (Ps. 28:7)

Put on the full armor of God, so that you will be able
to stand firm against the schemes of the devil.
(Eph. 6:11)

Seeking Humility Means Accepting God's Design for Our Lives

We seek humility when, in prayer, we acknowledge the
wisdom of how God designed us.

For You formed my inward parts;
You wove me in my mother's womb.
I will give thanks to You, for I am fearfully and
wonderfully made;
wonderful are Your works,
And my soul knows it very well.
My frame was not hidden from You
When I was made in secret,
And skillfully formed in the depths of the earth;
Your eyes have seen my formless substance;

And in Your book were all written
The days that were ordained for me,
When as yet there was not one of them.
(Ps. 139:13–16)

We seek humility when we accept the way God has gifted us and cease conforming to the world's mold rather than God's creative design and holy will.

For through the grace given to me I say to everyone among you not to think more highly of himself than he ought to think; but to think so as to have sound judgment, as God has allotted to each a measure of faith. (Rom. 12:3)

Seeking Humility Means Accepting God's Promises

As you pray, you can accept that you are gifted and be humble at the same time.

As each one has received a special gift, employ it in serving one another as good stewards of the multi-faceted grace of God. (1 Peter 4:10)

As you pray, you can accept that you are secure and be humble at the same time.

What then shall we say to these things? If God is for us, who is against us? (Rom. 8:31)

As you pray, you can accept that you are loved and be humble at the same time.

For I am convinced that neither death, nor life, nor angels, nor principalities, nor things present, nor things to come, nor powers, nor height, nor depth, nor any other created thing will be able to separate us from the love of God that is in Christ Jesus our Lord. (Rom. 8:38–39)

As you pray, you can accept that God strengthens you and enables you to be confident and be humble at the same time.

I can do all things through Him who strengthens me. (Phil. 4:13)

As you pray, you can accept that you are worthy of God's blessing and be humble because Christ has graciously earned every blessing for us.

> But love your enemies and do good, and lend, expecting nothing in return; and your reward will be great, and you will be sons of the Most High; for He Himself is kind to ungrateful and evil people. (Luke 6:35)

> Blessed be the God and Father of our Lord Jesus Christ, who has blessed us with every spiritual blessing in the heavenly places in Christ. (Eph. 1:3)

Review the points of this chapter, and ask God to reveal any prideful resistance. Ask for the grace to repent of this and believe Him for the greater grace that He promises (James 4:6). God will graciously empower and bless every effort of your seeking humility—even your seeking to associate with the humble (Prov. 16:19; Rom. 12:16). E. M. Bounds said: "Humility of the heart is what brings the praying soul near to God. Lowliness of mind is what gives wings to prayer."[1] This humility enables our prayers to soar to God's ears.

You are set free to experience the Spirit's gracious motivation and enablement in your prayer life:

- As you cease trying to be God
- As you admit your need and use these needs to propel you to seek God in prayer
- As you accept His design for your life and trust His wisdom in the way He has gifted you
- As you humbly accept and believe His gracious promises as you pray

For Personal and Group Reflection

Examine the four main headings titled "Seeking Humility Means . . ." Ask God to point out any prideful resistance, and write down what He shows you.

Chapter Five

Replacing Our Selfish Interest and Criticalness with Love

In my book *A Journey to Victorious Praying*, I tell the story of John Hyde, a missionary to India.

> John Hyde had a heavy burden for a pastor in India. He began to pray for him and with great concern began to tell God how cold and indifferent this pastor was and how he was a great hindrance to God's work. While John prayed, God convicted him for his critical spirit and cooperating with the "accuser of the brethren" and not with the Holy Spirit. As he was meditating on Philippians 4:8 he learned

that he needed to dwell not only on things that were true, but also lovely and even worthy of praise. . . . "Is there anything I can praise You for in this pastor's life?" John asked God. He was reminded of many things that he could genuinely praise God for in the pastor's life. What was the result? He later learned that the pastor's heart had experienced revival at the exact time of his praise. Commit your concern to the Spirit of God and let Him motivate and guide you as you take it to the Lord in prayer. His motivating love is radically different than the critical spirit generated by the "accuser of the brethren."[1]

How can God enable us to experience the Spirit's loving motivation in our prayer lives? We can glean four key principles of guidance from Romans 9:1–5.

1. Seek to live in integrity before God (Rom. 9:1)

As you read Paul's writings, you will see the phrases "before Him" and "God is my witness." This practice of living in God's presence is described by the apostle John as "walking in the light" and means to live openly, honestly, and transparently before God (1 John 1:7) with a clear conscience, forsaking any known sin (Prov. 28:13) or dubious habits (Rom. 14:23). Living in this integrity protects and guards you from being open to the deception of false burdens and taking on sacrifices that are not prompted or energized by God but result in dead works. It also enables you to enjoy His presence and rest in the assurance that you are never alone (Heb. 13:5–6).

The story goes that Martin Luther was asked one day, "Where would you be if all your followers were to leave you?" The German reformer replied, "I would be right in the presence of God."

2. Surrender your heart to the Lord (Rom. 9:2)

The term "heart" refers to the control center of our life. It is used not only of our emotions, but also of our mind—"thoughts of their hearts" (Gen. 6:5) and our will—"as he has decided in his heart" (2 Cor. 9:7). God is able to place His ministry and prayer burdens on the heart that is surrendered to Him. We observe in Romans 9:2 that Paul had "great sorrow and unceasing grief" in his heart as he contemplated his fellow Israelites. This is what led to his prayers for them, which were an expression of his heart's desire (Rom. 10:1).

Not every ministry or prayer burden will be assigned to you. In the words of Richard Foster, "If the idea is accompanied with a sense of dread, then probably you should set it aside. God will lead someone else to pray for the matter."[2] It is incredibly liberating to realize that God does not assign everything that needs to be prayed for to you personally. Although we need to be willing to receive any prayer burden, not all of these will be given to us, nor will we be given the grace to carry all of them. Saying no to what has not been assigned to us allows us to say yes and experience God's gracious enablement to what has been given to us. However, if it is an inner compassionate concern that is energized by God's Spirit, it may indeed be a prayer project for you.

Years ago, during a sermon at Moody Bible Institute, missionary J. Oswald Sanders described a call as "a growing conviction as you become acquainted with the facts."[3] Another missionary, Sammy Tippit, gives us this advice: "Find a large group of people and walk among them silently praying, 'God, let me see these people as You see them. Let me feel what You feel for them.' Do this regularly and consistently. The Holy Spirit will begin to melt your heart."[4] As you pray, God will show you how to cooperate with Him. For Paul, it meant accepting God's call to be the apostle to the Gentiles and provoking his fellow Israelites to jealously desire the blessings of God that they observed on the Gentiles who trusted in their Messiah (Rom. 11:13–14).

3. Look to the Lord to empower you to lovingly respond to the prayer burden He gives you (Rom. 9:3)

In Paul's life, we see how the Spirit put in him a sacrificial love for those who violently opposed him. Just as Christ became a curse for our sins when He died for us (Gal. 3:13; 2 Cor. 5:21), so the Spirit empowered Paul to almost wish that he could bear their judgment and go to hell that his enemies could go to heaven. A World War II veteran asked, "Why is it so special that Jesus died for us? I gladly risked and sacrificed my life for my family and countrymen." The minister replied, "Would you have risked your life for Hitler's soldiers who tried to kill your family?" This kind of love is only authored by God. He will even give us this grace of love for the prayer burdens that He entrusts to us.

4. View those you pray for as those whom God desires to bless (Rom. 9:4–5)

As Paul looked out at his unbelieving fellow Israelites, he saw them as God's adopted people who had been entrusted with His glorious presence, His covenant promises, His law, the privilege of temple worship, and countless other promises. They were also the offspring of the famous patriarchs—Abraham, Isaac, and Jacob. And most of all, through them had come the Christ, who is described as being "over all, God blessed forever" (Rom. 9:5). Rather than viewing them only as ones who had opposed and rejected him and their glorious Messiah, he sees them as ones whom God desires to bless.

The most challenging person to love in your life may unlock the greatest blessing as you obey God in that relationship. Remember that no one in our lives is more deserving of God's wrath than we are. Worship God because He loves us so much and delivered us from that judgment, and because He is "kind to ungrateful and evil people" (Luke 6:35). Trust Him to see others also from this perspective!

All these suggestions are things each one of us can do as we depend on the Holy Spirit. We all are tempted like praying missionary John Hyde to respond in unloving judgmentalism as we encounter things that disturb us—even things that should disturb us. However, there is a path that can lead us to experience God's love in and through our lives.

- Seek to live in integrity before God by turning your temptations into conversations with God and even intercessions for others. (This will be further explained in the next chapters.)
- Surrender your heart to the Lord and be open to any prayer burden that He gives you. What He gives you will be accompanied by His motivating and enabling grace.
- Look to the Lord to empower you to lovingly respond to the prayer burden He gives you.
- View those God directs you to pray for—even the very difficult assignments—as those whom God desires to bless.

As you follow these principles, only eternity will be able to tell the story of the fruit that will result from your obedience, which He alone can and will motivate and enable.

For Personal and Group Reflection

Reread the experience of John Hyde. Ask God to show you in what way you are praying about the difficulties of your life in cooperating with the accuser of our brothers and sisters and not the Holy Spirit.

As you surrender your heart to the Lord, write down the ministry burdens and prayer burdens that you sense God has given to you.

Chapter Six

Turning Our Temptations into Conversations with God

Temptation is a common experience for everyone (see 1 Cor. 10:13). It is a deceitful invitation to fulfill a legitimate need in a destructive way. In a later chapter, we will explain how the Spirit can help guide us in sharing the true desires of our heart with God. In that chapter, we will examine C. S. Lewis's quote, "The prayer preceding all prayers is 'May it be the real I who speaks. May it be the real Thou that I speak to.'"[1]

Living and praying with integrity involves turning these temptations into conversations with God. If you are experiencing the temptation to fear and be anxious, and not talking to God about this fear and anxiety, you are not praying (Ps. 34:4; Phil. 4:6–7). If you are letting the hurt in your heart turn into angry bitterness and not trusting God to heal that hurt, you are not praying. If your conscience is troubled and confused with guilty accusations and you are not bringing that struggle in the light to God, you are not praying (1 John 1:7).

Turning your temptations into open, honest, and transparent conversations with God is the only way to overcome their deceit. These temptations deceitfully appealed to the pain of your unmet longings by offering some temporary pleasure. What is hidden in their appeal is the fact that this temporary pleasure will result in guilt, bondage, and even intensified pain that makes one vulnerable to the next deceitful temptation. This is the path to the cycle of addiction.

For this reason, one needs to heed God's daily exhortation, which He can provide through a healthy community to overcome this deceit (see Heb. 3:13). These are people we allow to speak truthfully to us; people the Lord can use to point out blind spots and areas of our life where we need to make adjustments. In prayer, you can invite the Lord to show you any way that you have developed an unhealthy pattern of following a deceitful temptation. Regarding sexual temptation, or any other God-given drive that the temptation appeals to, do not view the drive as a wolf that needs to be caged. Rather, view it as a seeing-eye dog to lead you to Jesus.

> When You said, "Seek My face," my heart said to You, "I shall seek Your face, LORD." (Ps. 27:8)

> Therefore let's approach the throne of grace with confidence, so that we may receive mercy and find grace for help at the time of our need. (Heb. 4:16)

As you respond in this way, any destructive temptation can be channeled into the experience of a genuine delight in God (Ps. 37:4).

As stated earlier, one way to pray your heart is to share your temptations with the Lord. A temptation appeals to a legitimate need and offers to meet that need in an unrighteous way. The temporary satisfaction of pleasure that comes from yielding to the temptation will eventually lead to not only guilt but an intensified need in your heart. This is so vividly expressed in Nathan's rebuke of David in 2 Samuel 12:7–14:

Nathan then said to David, "You are the man! This is what the LORD God of Israel says: 'It is I who anointed you as king over Israel, and it is I who rescued you from the hand of Saul. I also gave you your master's house and your master's wives into your care, and I gave you the house of Israel and Judah; and if that had been too little, I would have added to you many more things like these! Why have you despised the word of the LORD by doing evil in His sight? You have struck and killed Uriah the Hittite with the sword, you have taken his wife as your wife, and you have slaughtered him with the sword of the sons of Ammon. Now then, the sword shall never leave your house, because you have despised Me and have taken the wife of Uriah the Hittite to be your wife.' This is what the LORD says: 'Behold, I am going to raise up evil against you from your own household; I will even take your wives before your eyes and give them to your companion, and he will sleep with your wives in broad daylight. Indeed, you did it secretly, but I will do this thing before all Israel, and in open daylight.'" Then David said to Nathan, "I have sinned against the LORD." And Nathan said to

David, "The LORD also has allowed your sin to pass; you shall not die. However, because by this deed you have shown utter disrespect for the LORD, the child himself who is born to you shall certainly die."

Note how God expresses that he has showered David with many things and has many other gifts to give to him. David is then rebuked for not coming to the Lord to satisfy the thirst of his heart as he lusted after Bathsheba and in fear murdered her husband. Look at how Jesus invites us to bring our thirsty hearts to Him. Our times of temptation can be used to aid us in getting in touch with these thirsts.

Now on the last day, the great day of the feast, Jesus stood and cried out, saying, "If anyone is thirsty, let him come to Me and drink. The one who believes in Me, as the Scripture said, 'From his innermost being will flow rivers of living water.'" (John 7:37–38)

As you develop this pattern of turning every temptation into conversation with God, the Lord Himself can replace any devilish despair with His hope. May He also give you His guidance in regard to any way that you are making provisions for a wrong response and replace this pattern with an obedient response that we will explore in the next chapter.

> But put on the Lord Jesus Christ, and make no provision for the flesh in regard to its lusts. (Rom. 13:14)

> Now flee from youthful lusts and pursue righteousness, faith, love, and peace with those who call on the Lord from a pure heart. (2 Tim. 2:22)

For Personal and Group Reflection

What temptation in your life is drawing you to the Lord?

What insight for your life do you learn from Nathan's rebuke of David (2 Sam. 12:7–14; see John 7:37–39)?

Chapter Seven

Turning Our Temptations into Intercession for Others

I will always remember a very insightful conversation with a dear man of God at the conclusion of an early Sunday morning Bible study. He told me how a gentleman on the West Coast was leading many to Christ and away from a variety of past bondages, instructing them how to live in freedom. He wanted these new converts to know that even after salvation, they would be tempted to go back to these wrong patterns. He gave them some helpful guidance in how they could respond and experience victory.

I had previously experienced great freedom in turning my temptations into conversations with God. The insight that I gained that Sunday morning provided another very helpful truth that blesses me every day. I have had the privilege of sharing this with thousands of others who have also found great help in following this insight.

The first step is to identify and confess your most persistent and challenging temptation. It is not a sin to be tempted, as Jesus Himself was tempted in all ways as we are, yet without sin (Heb. 4:15). Let me encourage you to take out a sheet of paper and write down the temptation. Afterward, ask God to give you a prayer burden that every time you are tempted in this way, you will be prompted to pray this prayer request. Let it be a prayer request that will damage Satan's kingdom as God answers this prayer! In this way, you are using the temptation to sin to become a motivation to pray in a very strategic way.

Imagine the power of a prayer said by a father or mother who, every time they are tempted to have an impure thought, then used these temptations as a prompting to pray for the purity of their children. What if every time you were tempted to be discouraged and even to despair, you prayed that God would give encouragement and hope to your spiritual leaders? A number of years ago, when I was speaking at a missions conference at Moody Church in Chicago, I encouraged the people to adopt a nation as a prayer focus when they were tempted and to ask God to send laborers into that harvest field (Matt. 9:38). It might even be helpful for you to start this practice with a prayer partner and pledge in God's strength to pray for each other every time you are tempted.

Continue to turn all your temptations into conversations with God and look to Him who has the infinite resources of heaven to satisfy your deepest longings (John 7:37–38). Be alert to any way that He prompts you to obey Him. The blessing of turning these temptations into intercession for others is that you can use your weakness to experience His power in humble and compassionate intercession. You can easily get tired of saying no to temptation if you're not also using the opportunity to say yes to His promptings to pray for others.

Only eternity will reveal the fruit of your willingness to obey God in this way! Would you be willing to join me in adopting the readers of this book as one of your prayer requests? Every time we are tempted, we can pray for all who read this book to experience hope and power in their most persistent temptation.

For Personal and Group Reflection

Write down your most persistent temptation, and then write down a strategic prayer that you will pray when you are tempted in this way.

Chapter Eight

Overcoming a Worried and Troubled Heart with One That Glorifies God

Martha was a dear woman who graciously welcomed Christ and His disciples into her home. However, she did not enjoy the visit! She was involved in a worthwhile ministry, but in the midst of her work, she found herself distracted, worried, and troubled (Luke 10:40–41). God loves us in our most distracted, worried, and bothered condition, but He loves us so much that He has not sentenced us to live that way.

Jesus did not rebuke Martha for her service or hard work. He did rebuke her, and will also correct us when our worried and troubled attitude causes us to:

1. Doubt His love—"Lord, do you not care . . ."
   (Luke 10:40).
2. Be critical of others—". . . that my sister has left
   me . . ." (Luke 10:40).
3. Feel isolated—". . . to do the serving by myself"
   (Luke 10:40).
4. Have a demanding spirit toward Christ—"Tell
   her to help me" (Luke 10:40).

Mary was Martha's sister and received a commendation from the Lord. She is not commended for not helping or being lazy, because neither is true. The text seems to imply that she had helped her sister before she took her seat at the Lord's feet. She is commended, and so we can also receive Christ's encouragement when we . . .

1. are "also seated" (Luke 10:39)—attentive and
   listening to the Lord.
2. are "at the Lord's feet" (Luke 10:39)—under His
   authority and willing to do anything He asks. This
   obedience starts by continually casting all our cares
   upon the Lord (1 Peter 5:6–7; Phil. 4:6–7).[1]

3. have "chosen the good part" (Luke 10:42)—
   enjoying Christ's presence, which is the real prize.
4. hope in that "which shall not be taken away"
   (Luke 10:42)—it leads to eternal fruit, which is
   a result of abiding in the Lord (John 15:5) and
   laboring with the Lord (Ps. 127:1–2).

The story in Luke 10:38–42 is placed between the two well-known passages of Scripture: Luke 10:25–37, the story of the good Samaritan, and Luke 11:1–13, the story of our Lord's teaching on prayer. The inspired placement of this passage is for thematic reasons, as the events in the passages are not in chronological order. What is the intended message of this thematic placement of the story between these passages? The attitude of Martha that our loving Lord rebukes is what hinders one's ability to see and meet the needs of others, as seen in the story of the good Samaritan. This distracted, worried, and troubled spirit, when unchecked, also hinders one's communion with the Lord in prayer. On the other hand, the attitude of Mary, which our gracious Lord commends, is a picture of abiding in the Lord and enables one to cooperate with God in compassionate acts of service and to enjoy the "good part" of communion with God in prayer.

It is the Lord who can transform our lives from seeking to "make a name for ourselves" (Gen. 11:4) to the cry of Psalm 115:1—"Not to us, LORD, not to us, but to Your name give glory." Seeking God's glory is choosing the good part, because God's glory is the revealed attributes of His glorious person. Seeking God's glory is what will ignite faith in our prayers. Listen to our Lord's rebuke when one's pursuit goes the other direction: "How can you believe, when you receive glory from one another and you do not seek the glory that is from the one and only God?" (John 5:44).

I will never forget hearing the late Dr. Bill Bright's words: "If all you desire is the glory of God and the well-being of others, it is impossible to ask God for too much." Maybe that is what the late Dallas Willard was getting at when he told a group of pastors that the most important work of a pastor was to pray for the success of the other churches in his area!

To seek God's glory does not in any way mean that we ourselves do not need or desire His blessing. It just gives a deeper motivation for desiring these blessings. "God be gracious to us and bless us, and cause His face to shine upon us—Selah. That Your way may be known on the earth, Your salvation among all nations" (Ps. 67:1–2); and "God blesses us, so that all the ends of the earth may fear Him" (Ps. 67:7).

Paul's desire to experience God's blessing in his life and in his ministry to the Gentiles was that his fellow Israelites would be moved to jealously desire what only God can provide (Rom. 11:13–14). In fact, God desires to make each of His children an object lesson to show for all eternity how gracious and kind He is—"so that in the ages to come He might show the boundless riches of His grace in kindness toward us in Christ Jesus" (Eph. 2:7).

Look at the kindness of God's glory:

- He glorifies His name by guiding His people in paths of righteousness (Ps. 23:3).
- He glorifies His name by graciously and mercifully forgiving our sin, which is great but not greater than His grace (Ps. 25:11).
- He leads His people to find rest to make for Himself a glorious name (Isa. 63:14).

The pursuit of God's glory as we pray is only possible in the enablement of the Holy Spirit. Open your life up to the Spirit who was sent for the purpose of glorifying Christ.

Listen to our Lord's Word: "He will glorify Me, for He will take from Mine and will disclose it to you" (John 16:14). The clear teaching of the Scripture is that only Jesus' liberating death on the cross can free one from living only for oneself (2 Cor. 5:14–15).[2] Furthermore, the only way to experience this liberation in our daily lives is by dependence on the Holy Spirit (Gal. 5:16).[3] It is for this reason that Jesus sent His Spirit as our "Helper" in every way we would need it. In His strength, we can live and pray for His glory.

This is our hope and one of the reasons that God commands us to pray in the Holy Spirit. I have previously instructed thousands of others to do what I am now asking you to do as you conclude this chapter. Put your finger on Galatians 1:24, and petition God to so work in your life as you pray that many others would glorify God because of what God has and is doing in and through you.

"And they were glorifying God because of me" (Gal. 1:24).

For Personal and Group Reflection

Explain how the story of Mary and Martha (Luke 10:38–42) relates to the passage that precedes it (Luke 10:30–37) and the passage that follows it (Luke 11:1–13).

Write down your response to Bill Bright's quote, "If all you desire is the glory of God and the well-being of others, it is impossible to ask God for too much."

Chapter Nine

Opening Up Our Lives to God's Cleansing and Restoration

Desiring to experience the motivation of the Spirit in our prayer lives certainly involves dealing with matters that are clearly grieving (Eph. 4:30) and quenching the Spirit (1 Thess. 5:9). Here are a few Scriptures that may provide a helpful guide for us:

- "If I regard wickedness in my heart, the Lord will not hear" (Ps. 66:18). Regarding wickedness in our heart involves covering our sin and not confessing and forsaking it (see Prov. 28:13).
- "He who shuts his ear to the outcry of the poor will also call out himself, and not be answered"

(Prov. 21:13). This refers to a clear quenching of God's guidance and prompting to give to those in need.

- "One who turns away his ear from listening to the Law, even his prayer is an abomination" (Prov. 28:9). This verse shows us that prayer is not a substitute for obedience.
- "Whenever you stand praying, forgive, if you have anything against anyone, so that your Father who is in heaven will also forgive you for your offenses" (Mark 11:25). Harboring bitterness in our hearts hinders our experience of God's continual cleansing of our sin and fellowship with God (see 1 John 1:7, 9).
- "You husbands in the same way, live with your wives in an understanding way, as with someone weaker, since she is a woman; and show her honor as a fellow heir of the grace of life, so that your prayers will not be hindered" (1 Peter 3:7). We can't compartmentalize our prayer life from the rest of our life. We can't live compromising lives with our spouse without hindering our prayer lives.[1]

I remember reading years ago of a pharmacist who wrongly filled a customer's prescription from her eye doctor. As the customer applied the wrong medicine, it resulted in an alarming and damaging swelling of her eyes. When she reported this to her doctor, he was shocked and recognized that the wrong medication had been dispensed.

The woman went back and told the pharmacist, who was also alarmed at the condition of her eyes, and he promptly gave her the correct medicine. However, her swelling worsened, and she periodically visited the pharmacist over the next four months and showed him her deteriorating condition.

Aware of his moral and legal liability, the desperate pharmacist set aside a weekend to the Lord and prayed for her healing. During this time, God brought to his attention an area of sensual bondage in his life that he needed to confess to his wife and forsake. This would be the most humbling thing he had ever done. When he confessed his secret sin to his wife, she informed him that she had known that something was wrong and had decided to leave him and take the three children. However, she realized that the man who was talking to her now was different from the man she wanted to leave. In fact, she decided to stay and work to make their marriage successful. The account I read also stated that the woman with the eye condition came to see him the next day and reported that her eyes had begun to heal.

It would be wrong to assume that every scenario will have this happy ending. However, we can be sure that God always blesses a repentant heart and is a restoring God. He also may want to give us more than we know how to ask. In this case, not only did God grant healing to the woman's eyes, but also healing to the pharmacist's marriage and family. Look at the prophecy of Ezekiel 36 as it speaks of the future act of the restoration of God's people. It is a strong encouragement to believe God to honor His own name in restoring our lives and the lives of others for whom we pray. We see in chapter 36 that God took His people from captivity back to the land (the place of blessing) to honor His name and experience His cleansing restoration:

> "When they came to the nations where they went, they profaned My holy name, because it was said of them, 'These are the people of the LORD, yet they have come out of His land.' But I had concern

for My holy name, which the house of Israel had profaned among the nations where they went.

"Therefore, say to the house of Israel, 'This is what the Lord GOD says: "It is not for your sake, house of Israel, that I am about to act, but for My holy name, which you have profaned among the nations where you went. I will vindicate the holiness of My great name which has been profaned among the nations, which you have profaned among them. Then the nations will know that I am the Lord," declares the Lord GOD, "when I show Myself holy among you in their sight. For I will take you from the nations, and gather you from all the lands; and I will bring you into your own land. Then I will sprinkle clean water on you, and you will be clean; I will cleanse you from all your filthiness and from all your idols. Moreover, I will give you a new heart and put a new spirit within you; and I will remove the heart of stone from your flesh and give you a heart of flesh.""" (vv. 20–26)

The same God can also glorify His name in our lives as we humbly seek Him for our restoration.

Prayer is not a substitute for obedience. Years ago, I discovered these four questions from Life Action Ministries, and I have shared them below to aid each of us in assessing which areas of our lives may need adjusting:

1. Identify one area of your life in which your full obedience would tear down all barriers between you and God's blessing.
2. Is there anything God wants you to start doing?
3. Is there anything God wants you to stop doing?
4. Is there any reason not to do what God wants?[2]

The four challenges that Evan Roberts gave that ignited the spark of the Welsh Revival are a part of my regular prayer life. Here are his four challenges that will aid you in your own prayer life:

1. Confess and forsake any known sin.
2. Confess and forsake any doubtful habit (Rom. 14:23).
3. Obey the promptings of the Spirit in your secret, private life.
4. Openly confess Christ in your public life.[3]

God has mercifully provided inspired patterns for us to learn from as we seek to be fully restored to our Lord. Perhaps the following insights that a godly pastor[4] has provided about confession from Psalm 51 will help you as it has me:

- True confession relies on God's mercy (v. 1).
- True confession takes full responsibility (vv. 2–3).
- True confession sees the root of our sin (v. 5).
- True confession longs for a sustained life of obedience (vv. 10, 12).
- True confession longs for a return of the enjoyment and experience of God's presence (v. 11).
- True confession longs for useful ministry in the future (vv. 14–15).
- True confession is fueled by brokenness (vv. 16–17).
- True confession leads to joy (vv. 8, 12).
- True personal confession can lead to corporate revival (v. 18).

God is a God of hope and desires to honor His name and fully restore you to His place of blessing. God delights to forgive; we are not the ones willing Him to forgive us. He has to make *us* willing to seek His forgiveness. And as you genuinely seek God, there eventually comes an end to the self-examination process. In other words, God is eager to restore a repentant heart. He is the One who makes us willing to seek His cleansing. Let Him examine you and also lead you to joy and the everlasting way.

> Search me, God, and know my heart;
> Put me to the test and know my anxious thoughts;
> And see if there is any hurtful way in me,
> And lead me in the everlasting way. (Ps. 139:23–24)

God will honor a repentant heart. He longs to restore and bless even His disobedient people as they turn to Him (see Ps. 81:11–16). To a truly repentant heart, God can even work good out of our past sin. Our past sin is not good, but God can overrule it for good (Rom. 8:28).[5] Trust Him to even place His healing hand on hurts that your sin has caused.

Yes, sin in all our lives has injured others in some way. Even the role model of our faith, Abraham, was struck with fear that led to his lying about his wife in calling her his sister. When King Abimelech made advances toward beautiful Sarah, God did what He said He would do: "I will bless those who bless you, and he who curses you

I will curse" (Gen. 12:3). In this case, He closed the wombs of all the households of Abimelech. However, when Abraham repented and prayed, "God healed Abimelech and his wife and his female slaves, so that they gave birth to children" (Gen. 20:17).[6]

Let God complete your story. Take a moment to reflect on this chapter, believing God for full restoration and believing Him to place His healing hands on the hurts that you have caused.

For Personal and Group Reflection

Write down your response to the four questions cited in this chapter:

1. Identify one area of your life in which your full obedience would tear down all barriers between you and God's blessing.

2. Is there anything God wants you to start doing?

3. Is there anything God wants you to stop doing?

4. Is there any reason not to do what God wants?

As you answer these four questions above, meditate on the truth that God glorifies His name in restoring His people to the place of His full blessing (Ezek. 36:20–26).

What past sin that you have confessed and forsaken do you need to trust God to overrule for His glory and your ultimate good?

What past hurt that your sin has caused in others do you need to trust God to put His healing touch upon?

Part 3

EXPERIENCING THE GUIDANCE OF THE HOLY SPIRIT

Chapter Ten

Getting in Touch with Our Hearts

Have you ever lost the joy of corporate worship? Have you ever looked at your time in your Sunday services as only an obligation? In my childhood, before I knew the Lord, I viewed attending church as a ticket that permitted me to enjoy the other activities of the rest of the day.

Even as a genuine believer, I experienced a season in which I no longer had an anticipation of meeting with the living God in my Sunday worship service. I was present in the services and faithfully sought to participate, but my heart was not engaged. This season lasted longer than I want to remember. Although you can blame others for your dry experience, you will never get out of it without seeking the Lord and taking personal responsibility. I set aside a day to seek the Lord for His solution.

I realized my need to prepare for the Lord's Day. God gave me a simple plan that has aided me for more than forty years now. I look at my upcoming week and consider my concerns—present and future responsibilities, relational concerns, guidance I need in decisions I need to make, etc. Then I write down these concerns on a sheet of paper in preparation for the Lord's Day. I carry them into church even if I am speaking that day. The conviction that came out of seeking the Lord for resolution was this: there will never be a Lord's Day that I do not share my heart with Him. After the Sunday service, on that same sheet of paper, I write down any insight I have received in response to the concerns I shared with the Lord. I now have hundreds of sheets of paper with these notations. While they may be worthless to anyone else, they are a reminder to me that God is my personal heavenly Father who knows my name and address and is eager to aid me in all the areas of my life.

Praying in the Spirit involves being open to the Spirit helping you examine your heart by identifying and professing your true desires and concerns. Sometimes we are carrying burdens, fears, and anger that we are not even aware of. During my growing up, if someone had asked me, "Are you angry?" or "Are you fearful?" I would have said no and not intentionally been lying. However, I would have been lying because I had not learned how to share my heart. Rather than viewing prayer as only another duty and responsibility, see it as a gracious gift of a loving God who wants to aid you opening your heart to Him. I do not want to leave you with the impression that prayer is simply about helping us feel good. It is about God helping us deal with the fears and hurts, and reveal the desires of our soul. It is not a mere human activity but one in which the Spirit of God comes to assist and empower us to pray!

How God works is not a complete mystery because He has told us how He works. When God wants to do something, He puts a prayer concern on someone's heart. As people respond in prayer to what God has put on their hearts, His work is set in motion (Isa. 62:6–7; Matt. 9:35–36). I teach at a school that was founded by D. L. Moody. One day he felt drawn to his knees and prayed, "God, give me this land for my school." That is a vivid reminder of God's faithfulness as I see and daily experience the concrete answer to this prayer.

As God was resurrecting my dead prayer life and teaching me how to avail myself of the Spirit's help, I sensed the Lord seeking to slow me down on the inside. I realized that I even started my days with an inward spirit of hurry and rush. I had learned to diligently go about my work, but not in a way that I enjoyed the Lord in the midst of my work. Years ago, I read a statement by John Wesley, the early Methodist leader, that said, "Although I am always in haste, I am never in a hurry. I never do more than I can do without perfect calmness of spirit."[1] That describes a diligence that is authored by the Holy Spirit. A spirit of hurry is the death of prayer!

For a brief time, I took some drastic measures to begin my day in a peaceful spirit. I would take a train to Chicago that arrived at least two hours before I needed to be at work. I would go to a restaurant where no one knew me and sit quietly and make sure I was fully obeying 1 Peter 5:7, casting all my cares to the Lord who truly cares for me.

As you seek God in acknowledging and declaring what is on your heart, be open to what He may be putting on your heart. Let me briefly share a short excerpt of a couple of personal experiences that I share in my book *A Journey to Victorious Praying: Finding Discipline and Delight in Your Prayer Life.*[2]

God will not give any of us every prayer burden. Our responsibility is to present our lives to Him and let Him place on our hearts the prayer burden He has for us. One routine Saturday morning, I arose to have some time with the Lord. I was quite ready to go about my errands for the day, but I had a great uneasiness in my spirit. Attempting to be sensitive to what I had ignored too much of my life, I sat silently before the Lord and asked Him if there was anything else He desired me to talk to Him about. A couple of things came to mind, and then there was the thought of "safety." After I prayed for God to keep me safe that day, I felt a liberty in my spirit to go into the day. Four hours later as I was driving, another car pushed me into the lane of oncoming traffic. Somehow, I avoided contact with the cars on either side of me, and all I could think was "safety." I praised God for how He had prepared me for this in prayer and confessed to Him the many times I had ignored Him by living in a spirit of rush. God knows how to prepare us for all that is ahead as we seek to be attentive to Him.

On another occasion, I was taking a walk with my wife, and we both had a sense of the need to pray for a neighbor boy whom we deeply love. Jeff has been a big brother to my three boys, and we love him as if he were our own son. We poured out our hearts for him in prayer as we walked. God knew that that night Jeff would be rushed to the hospital with an injury to his eye, and I would have the opportunity to sit with his parents as we trusted God to deal with the situation. Praise God all went well, and God once again showed me that He can intervene in our agenda and give us a prayer burden to prepare us for what is ahead.

I do not want to give you the impression that this happens every time I pray, for it certainly does not. However, it is necessary to be open to it. Many times, I have taken walks and asked the Lord to bring to my mind anything for which He would have me pray.[3]

May God richly bless each of us as we open ourselves up to the Holy Spirit, who promises to aid us in getting in touch with our hearts and will never lead us contrary to His Word, because He is the Spirit of truth.

For Personal and Group Reflection

Follow the counsel of this chapter and seek to use the Lord's Day to identify and profess the true desires and concerns of your heart. Even now, ask God to show you any adjustment you need to make in your life to stay in touch with your heart.

Write down anything that is between you and full obedience to 1 Peter 5:7.

Chapter Eleven

Praying Our Hearts

God's Spirit not only wants you to identify what is on your heart, He also wants to aid you in praying your heart. We are not adequate to live the Christian life in our own strength. We are to depend upon the Holy Spirit each step of the way (Gal. 5:16). Neither can we pray in our own strength, and for that reason, we have the command to depend on the Spirit as we pray (Eph. 6:18). The devil uses many schemes to not only distract you from prayer, but to convince you to despise it. One of these is to feel a responsibility to be involved in the activity of prayer, yet not be set free to express your heart.

When you are praying but ignoring the cries of your heart, you are not praying. As stated earlier, if you are fearful and anxious as you pray and not sharing your fear with the Lord, you are not praying. If you are angry and you are not talking to the Lord about the hurts of your heart, you are not praying. Notice the relationship between your heart's desire and prayer in these verses:

Lord, all my desire is before You; And my sighing is not hidden from You. (Ps. 38:9)

Brothers and sisters, my heart's desire and my prayer to God for them is for their salvation. (Rom. 10:1)

In an earlier chapter, I quoted C. S. Lewis, who said that the prayer that precedes all prayers is this: "May it be the real I who speaks. May it be the real Thou that I speak to." Colossians 4:2 tells us that prayer is a discipline that we are to devote ourselves to: "Devote yourselves to prayer, keeping alert in it with an attitude of thanksgiving."

However, as part of this discipline, be sure to stay attuned to what is in your heart. It is not at all wrong to use extensive prayer lists and reminders, but during your praying, be open to the guidance of the Spirit. As I was first learning this, I was praying through the matters for which I regularly interceded and discovered that my heart began to trouble me. I had to learn to abandon my previous agenda and get in touch with my heart and pray those concerns. The result was a whole new freedom to later pray for the other matters on my list. However, I also at times had to continue in the new agenda and trust God to raise up other people to pray for the other matters on my list I did not pray for.

I was set free by the testimony of one who told how he had tried to pray for every request that confronted him. His prayer life got nowhere until he realized that God was not asking him to pray for everything that needed to be prayed for. Remember that not every prayer burden will be assigned to you. I pray that you also will be set free to experience the grace to obey God's Spirit as He motivates you and leads you to pray your heart. Remember also that every temptation that seeks to lead you away from the Lord is His invitation to get in touch with the desire that the temptation is appealing to and share that desire with the Lord.

God sets His work in motion by putting a prayer burden on one's heart and enabling that person to pray in response to this burden. This is the truth that you can observe in the Old Testament (Isa. 62:6–7), where you'll notice in the verses below that God also encourages us to continually cry out to Him until He accomplishes His work:

On your walls, Jerusalem, I have appointed
  watchmen;
All day and all night they will never keep silent.
You who profess the LORD, take no rest for
  yourselves;
And give Him no rest until He establishes
And makes Jerusalem an object of praise on the
  earth.

You can also observe this principle in the New Testament (Matt. 9:36–38):

Seeing the crowds, He felt compassion for them, because they were distressed and downcast, like sheep without a shepherd. Then He said to His disciples, "The harvest is plentiful, but the workers are few. Therefore, plead with the Lord of the harvest to send out workers into His harvest."

In these verses we see God in the flesh in the person of Jesus, desiring to do a compassionate work. He proceeds to put His compassionate prayer burden on the hearts of His disciples. He then instructs them to respond to that prayer burden in order to see God work. It is this prayer that sets God's work in motion. God is the sovereign Master of the universe who works all things after the counsel of His will (Eph. 1:11), and He has chosen to work through prayer. What a privilege to humbly cooperate with Him!

For this reason, the priority of the gathered church is to pray.

> First of all, then, I urge that requests, prayers, inter-cession, and thanksgiving be made in behalf of all people, for kings and all who are in authority, so that we may lead a tranquil and quiet life in all godliness and dignity. (1 Tim. 2:1–2)

Notice the phrase "First of all." Prayer is the priority of the gathered church. There are numerous problems that Timothy is facing as he seeks to guide the church as Paul's representative in Ephesus. For that reason, he is instructed to let prayer be the first, and not last, resort. Timothy, like us today, was facing problems that only God could ulti-mately solve. If you were God's enemy, would you not try to keep His people so occupied that they could in no way be alert to the Spirit's guiding us to seek God in prayer for His divine help?

We all face many distractions just from the ordinary concerns of life. Jesus warned not to let the "worries of life" and wrong choices weigh us down so that we would not be left unprepared for His second coming (Luke 21:34). As you depend upon the Spirit, do not be surprised when He leads you into times of silence before Him in order to calm your heart. These times may seem to be very unproductive, but just the opposite is the truth. Let me illustrate that by one such experience in my own life in the early days of ministry.

At the conclusion of a chapel service, Dr. George Sweeting came to the pulpit and announced that classes would be canceled the next day. Classes would meet but only for the purpose of prayer. Students got excited and so did I. With that one announcement, I was relieved of all my preparations for my classes the next day.

As I pondered how to use that day, none of my plans, even my plan to fast, seemed to be appropriate. I lived across the street from a restaurant and started this special day by calling in a breakfast order and eating before boarding the train to Chicago. I sensed that the Lord wanted me to put down everything—even some of my normal disciplines—and be still and be quiet. As I went to my classes, I felt led to say as few words as possible—only "Let's seek God in prayer."

At the end of that day, I took my usual mile-and-a-half walk to the train. Being single at that time, I often ate a brief supper before I got on the train to my apartment. Usually, I ate at a place that served leftover lunch at a bargain price at supper. It was nothing special, but it did the job. On this day, I went instead to a nice restaurant and sat in a booth by myself. The waitress who took my order and delivered my meal said something to me that had never been said before. She said, "I go all over this restaurant, and I sense hurry and rush, and I come to your booth, and I sense peace." She said it three times. If you had seen me that day and inquired, "What did you do today?" I would have replied, "Very little, really nothing." You would not have been impressed. However, the Lord showed me that when you do nothing in obedience to Him, it will bear great fruit.

When we let Him slow us down from our "efforts" of seeking Him and serving Him, we can welcome and experience His manifest presence. This may be the key to listening to God and cooperating with Him as you seek to experience His gracious guidance in praying for the prayer burdens He has placed in your heart. May you obey God's Spirit today and follow His leading wherever it takes you as you pray your heart.

For Personal and Group Reflection

After reading this chapter, write down what God is putting on your heart to trust Him for.

Chapter Twelve

Praying Prayers That Affect Future Generations

Although the petition D. L. Moody made for land for a school was uttered before my life even started, I, along with countless others, daily benefit from the fruit of that prayer. It is a reminder to me each day to be open to what God desires me to trust Him for.

Bill Bright was studying for a Hebrew exam as a seminary student when God laid on his heart a ministry that would reach college students around the world. As he shared what he felt led to pray, one of his mentors even told him what he should call the ministry: "Call it Campus Crusade for Christ." That ministry (now called

Cru) is still proclaiming Christ around the world. My son and I both owe a great debt to this ministry, which God used in our lives during college.

Another notable illustration of a prayer that affected many others in the future comes from the life of Dr. John Perkins. Perkins is one of the leading spokesmen and leaders who has been instrumental in aiding others in the ministry of racial reconciliation and gospel ministry in the cities. He chose the path of love that shielded his soul from being ensnared with bitterness toward those who had wronged him in significant ways. I will never forget being in a small gathering and hearing Dr. Perkins share a story about his conversion. He was saved as an adult and had not even formally completed an elementary education. He was given a Bible and yearned to read and understand it. As he struggled to comprehend it, he began to despair for fear he just didn't have the ability to meet this challenge. At this point of despair, he cried out to God, "If You just open this book to me, I will do anything You ask to proclaim it." No one today would ever doubt that God answered that prayer. Not only does this man possess great spiritual discernment, he also has been awarded numerous honorary doctorates. That prayer continues to affect many generations. It would have never been prayed had not the Holy Spirit empowered John to cry out to God instead of giving in to the despair that the devil was scheming against him.

One of the most amazing prayer legacies that I've ever heard of is one Gil Beers related to me.[1] Beers is a prolific author of children's books. He has written more than two hundred books, which have sold over thirteen million copies. Even as he battled stomach cancer at the age of ninety-one, he never stopped writing love letters to his family. After having half of his stomach removed, he did not let that stop him from writing hundreds of letters to his wife, his four children, eleven grandchildren, and eighteen great-grandchildren.

Beers' wife's grandmother, Katherine Rudy, attracted little attention while she was alive. She was a stay-at-home wife in a small town in Iowa and married to a pastor of a struggling little church. While she was pregnant with her fourth child, her husband became extremely ill and died.

Katherine was left penniless and with four small children. She did not even have enough money to put a roof over her head, and so she moved in with her brother and his family. She accepted as the Spirit-appointed mission of her life to pray for her four children and her unborn grandchildren. Beers speaks of her four children, one of whom was his mother-in-law, as people who "glowed with the beautiful fragrance of the very presence of Christ."

Grandma Rudy left seventeen grandchildren, all Christians with Christian spouses who raised their children for the Lord. Beers shared their names with me and the significant impact of each one—a career missionary in Japan, a medical missionary in Africa, a leading businessman who worked with the Gideons, one who worked with Radio Bible Class, one who operated a Christian bookstore, a Christian musician, and a prolific Christian author were just some of their ministries. Grandma Rudy also left more than fifty great-grandchildren who also reflected a strong lineage of Christian ministry and missions.

A number of years ago, twelve of Grandma Rudy's seventeen grandchildren and their spouses met together and entered a covenant to pray for one another and their children and their grandchildren. They even developed a certificate for this covenant, which was signed by each of them.

In her life, Katherine Rudy might have been viewed as a pitiful woman unable to provide for her family. However, as she obeyed the Spirit's guidance and enablement to pray for her children and future grandchildren, she left a profound impact on her heritage. In fact, she continues to affect future generations. Each one of us can make our hearts available to receive any prayer burden that God will give us and respond to His motivation and enablement to pray accordingly. If you do, your future generations like Grandma Rudy's will rise and call you blessed.

For Personal and Group Reflection

Write down a prayer to pray for the future, even beyond your lifetime.

Part 4

EXPERIENCING
THE POWER
OF THE
HOLY SPIRIT

Chapter Thirteen

In Our Weakness

A former acquaintance, whom I will call Jim, left his lucrative career to enroll in a graduate program in Bible. He became quite legendary as a man of prayer. His maturity caused other students to look up to him and follow his leadership, seeking God in prayer under his guidance.

Later, while visiting me, Jim seemed obviously discouraged. He shared that during his pastoral internship he was visiting a sick woman in the hospital. In her extreme bitterness, she informed him, in no uncertain terms, that she had no desire for him or anyone else from the church to visit her.

Jim replied, "Can I just pray for you?"

She replied, "I don't care if you do or not. I didn't even ask you to come."

As Jim sought to pray for her, he began to cry. His tears were the only prayer he could muster. He reported this to the group in great distress and noted that he felt like a failure.

Jim's thoughts seemed to be going in the following direction, "I've left my career. I'm not a young man. I'm studying for a master's in Bible, and all I can do when I try to pray is cry like a baby. Tell me there is some hope for me!" What we later learned was that the woman had been struck by these compassionate tears. In fact, she had later opened her heart to the Lord and allowed God to deal with her bitterness, and even her health began to drastically improve.

The Holy Spirit helps us in our weakness. Our weakness is described as not knowing how to pray as we should. The Holy Spirit lends us a helping hand and prays the deep desires of our heart to the Father who graciously hears and answers them:

> In the same way the Spirit also helps our weakness; for we do not know how to pray as we should, but the Spirit Himself intercedes for us with groanings too deep for words; and He who searches the hearts knows what the mind of the Spirit is, because He intercedes for the saints according to the will of God. (Rom. 8:26–27)

In that moment, Jim could have leaned on his own understanding (Prov. 3:5). Instead, as he leaned upon the Spirit in his weakness of not knowing how to pray, the Spirit poured out tears of compassion. God heard the prayers of his heart that he did not know how to utter, and God used this prayer to heal this very bitter lady.

As the Spirit helps us in our weakness, He will plead our deep desires to the Father even if we do not know how to express them at that moment. Paul certainly earnestly prayed his desire that the painful thorn in the flesh be removed from him. God did not answer that request but did give him a deeper desire of his heart—to know God's grace and power to the fullest extent and be the most useful servant he could be. As we pray our desires, God's Spirit may be pleading a deeper desire that in our weakness we do not know how to pray (see 2 Cor. 12:7–10).

Some of the greatest gifts God has given me, and perhaps many of us, are prayers that He did not answer. My father-in-law was a brilliant civil engineer. He was the mastermind behind the underground tunnel system in Chicago. His greatest challenge as a businessman was assuming that everyone he worked for and with was as honest as he was. When I asked for his daughter's hand in marriage, I acknowledged that he knew what I did for a living and that both of us knew I would never earn large sums of money. He replied, "I love what you do and always want you to do it. I also plan to be very generous to all my children." He had a business project that was projected to channel millions of dollars to his heritage. Although he was always generous in his spirit to us, his business plan never materialized. The later years of his life were spent living on Social Security, and his needs were met but not in the way that he had anticipated. However, he died declaring that God had never disappointed him. He saw himself and all his family as richer by not having these millions of dollars being passed down. I greatly appreciated him as my father-in-law and have no doubt that God's Spirit had pleaded and answered the deeper desires of his heart.

Ruth Graham wrote a famous poem about how she would have greatly struggled in seeking to pray if she had been the mother of Joseph, the son of Jacob entrusted with slavery and prison. That would not have been her prayer for him! Nor would she have prayed, if she were Moses' mother, that her baby would be taken away from her. Nor as Daniel's mother, that he would be taken captive by Babylon!

The climax of the poem speaks of the agony she'd have felt if she were Mary. She would have prayed for anything but seeing Jesus crucified. However, with such prayers, Graham concludes, "My finite wisdom would assail Infinite Wisdom."[1]

For Personal and Group Reflection

Write your response to the poem by Ruth Graham and any application to your life.

Chapter Fourteen

In Believing God

In all areas of our life, we are to depend on the Holy Spirit (Gal. 5:16; Eph. 5:18). This includes our prayer life. Prayer is not to be only a human activity. For example:

- We need His enabling strength to submit to Jesus in prayer (Eph. 3:16).
- We need His power to persevere in prayer and get past a mere formalism and into real heartfelt prayer (Rom. 15:5).
- We need His power to resist Satan who seeks to lead us astray from the simplicity and purity of devotion to Christ (2 Cor. 11:3; James 4:7).

More could be said of each of these points, but I'm going to focus on another key area in which the Lord will aid us by His Spirit as we pray.

One day, I was asking God what it meant to be strong in the Lord, as Ephesians 6:10 states: "Finally, be strong in the Lord and in the strength of His might."

As I examined each New Testament use of the Greek word that is translated "be strong" in this verse, some key uses stood out. "With respect to the promise of God, he did not waver in unbelief but grew strong in faith, giving glory to God" (Rom. 4:20). The phrase "grew strong in faith" can be translated, "he was strengthened to believe." We need to realize that our faith is under spiritual attack. The environment of the world system is an atmosphere of unbelief. We daily hear the messages of the world as described in 1 John 2:16:

- Lust of the flesh—"If you have an urge for something, go after it."
- Lust of the eyes—"If something or someone looks appealing, go after it."
- Boastful pride of life—"Seek to exalt yourself; if you don't blow your horn, nobody else will."

When we respond to these messages without trusting and submitting to God's wisdom, great deceit and heartache will follow. For this reason, the apostle Paul alluded to this battle when he wrote to the Thessalonians that he wanted to "find out about your faith, for fear that the tempter might have tempted you" (1 Thess. 3:5). A believer is to look to the Lord who will strengthen him to believe. We do not need help to scheme or doubt, for we can do these by ourselves. We do need the Spirit's help to believe God. Our Lord is there to strengthen us even when we may find help in no one else. Notice how Paul testifies to this in the last book he wrote before his death.

> At my first defense no one supported me, but all deserted me; may it not be counted against them. But the Lord stood with me and *strengthened* me, so that through me the proclamation might be fully accomplished, and that all the Gentiles might hear; and I was rescued out of the lion's mouth. The Lord will rescue me from every evil deed and will bring me safely to His heavenly kingdom; to Him be the glory forever and ever. Amen. (2 Tim. 4:16–18)

The following story is a thrilling example of how the Spirit of God moved a young college student to believe God.[1]

Dr. Richard Harvey is one of the founders of Youth for Christ. He also served as a pastor, an evangelist, and a denominational leader. During his senior year in college, he observed an unusual answer to prayer that inspired him to courageously believe God on many future occasions in his life.

The largest and most popular course at the college that Harvey attended was a first-year chemistry class. Dr. Lee, the most renowned professor in the school, taught the class, and every year before Thanksgiving he lectured against prayer. He would conclude the lecture by offering a challenge to anyone who still believed in prayer. Harvey recalled the occasion when he wrote:

Then [Dr. Lee] would challenge, "Is there anybody here who still believes in prayer?" And he would say, "Before you answer, let me tell you what I am going to do and what I am going to ask you to do. I will turn around, take a glass flask and hold it at arm's length." Then he would continue, "If you believe that God answers prayer, I want you to stand and pray that when I drop this flask, it won't break. I want you to know that your prayers and the prayers of your parents and

Sunday school teachers and even the prayers of your own pastors cannot prevent this flask from breaking. If you wish to have them here, we will put this off until you return after the Thanksgiving recess."[2]

No one had ever stood up to Dr. Lee's challenge until a Christian freshman learned about it. He sensed that God had given him the conviction to stand up to the professor. Finally, the day came when the annual challenge was given. Dr. Lee made it in the same way that he had done for the past twelve years. The only difference was that this time the courageous freshman responded when asked if there was somebody who still believed in prayer. Harvey recalled the events that followed: "Well," said the professor, "this is most interesting. Now we will be most reverent while this young man prays." Then he turned to the young man, "Now you may pray."[3]

The young man lifted his countenance toward heaven and prayed, "God, I know that You can hear me. Please honor the name of Your Son, Jesus Christ, and honor me, Your servant. Don't let the flask break. Amen."[4]

Dr. Lee stretched his arm out as far as he could, opened his hand, and let the flask fall. It fell in an arc, hit the toe of Dr. Lee's shoe, rolled over, and did not break. There was no movement of air and there were no open windows. The class whistled, clapped, and shouted. And Dr. Lee ceased his annual lectures against prayer.

God's Spirit gave this young freshman the conviction to believe God. Although it is not the norm to believe God that a glass flask can be dropped and not break on a concrete floor, this freshman was given the faith of a David to stand up to a Goliath. God's honor was at stake, and He graciously worked through the faith of the pure-hearted freshman.

What does the Lord desire you to believe Him for today? Depend on the Spirit to strengthen you to believe Him as you seek Him.

As you seek Him, be assured that God is pleased when you trust Him (Heb. 11:6). Paul was in prison and not sure if he would live or die. However, in the mist of his uncertainty, he had absolute assurance of these two things. His "earnest expectation and hope" (which speaks of certainty) was ". . . not to be put to shame in anything, but that with all boldness, Christ will even now, as always, be exalted in my body, whether by life or by death" (Phil. 1:20).

What does it mean not to be put to shame? We find help in understanding this phrase by looking at our Lord's life as prophetically described in Isaiah 50:7. As He experienced the Father's help, He was not disgraced, and as He set His "face like flint," He knew that He would not be ashamed. Yes, Christ went to the cross and died for our sin and bore our shame; but He was not ashamed because the Father's purpose was accomplished.

In the same way, we, as Paul, can always pray with confidence for Christ's purpose to be accomplished and for Christ to be exalted during whatever uncertainty we are facing. When this happens, we are successful in God's eyes as our Lord's life provides the only true definition of success: "I glorified You on the earth by accomplishing the work which You have given Me to do" (John 17:4).

The challenge for each of us is to open every area of our life to the control of the Spirit. Fear is usually the root of our rebellion and our attempt to control our own lives.

In a similar way, we are to depend on the Spirit's control in every concern, task, and relationship of our life. Ask yourself, "Am I following the guidance found in Psalm 37:5, 'Commit your way to the LORD, trust also in Him, and He will do it'?" Are you doing anything that you have not first committed to Him? You cannot trust God for anything that you have not first surrendered to Him. As you trust Him, He will not make you irresponsible. He will guide you and empower you to do your part. However, be careful not to try to do what only God can do. He is the vine, and we are the branches (John 15:5).

Likewise, we are to respond to the control of the Spirit in our lives. Is our obedience up to date? Ensuring this will involve confessing our sins so that there is no disagreement between us and our Lord. We are to walk in the light (1 John 1:7), which means to live openly, honestly, and transparently for God and in His truth.

Note these three responsibilities that we have just cited to avail ourselves of the Spirit's help:

1. Open to His control
2. Dependent upon His control
3. Responsive to His control

Since the Holy Spirit inspired the writers of the Scripture to write God's Word, as you read it you will be aided in opening up your life to the Spirit's control. God's Word will also show you how to depend on the Spirit as well as how to respond to His promptings. The Holy Spirit is the Spirit of truth, and the fruit of His control is described in a comparable way to the fruit of the control of God's Word. Notice this similarity in the two Scriptures below. The first notes the control of the Spirit, and the second notes the control of God's Word.

> And do not get drunk with wine, in which there is debauchery, but be filled with the Spirit, speaking to one another in psalms and hymns and spiritual songs, singing and making melody with your hearts to the Lord; always giving thanks for all things in the name of our Lord Jesus Christ to our God and Father; and subject yourselves to one another in the fear of Christ. (Eph. 5:18–21)

> Let the word of Christ richly dwell within you, with all wisdom teaching and admonishing one another with psalms, hymns, and spiritual songs, singing with thankfulness in your hearts to God. (Col. 3:16)

As you are guided by the Spirit, He will enable you to believe Him to fulfill God's purpose and exalt Christ! Daily walk before God with this continual, submissive posture—"Lord, what do You want me to believe You for?"

Let's agree to pray for each other in the following ways:

- Believe God to use our lives to love His world. He who sits on His throne, judging righteously, will maintain this just cause. This is a just cause (1 Cor. 13:1–3)!

  "When my enemies turn back, they stumble and perish before You. For You have maintained my just cause; You have sat on the throne judging righteously" (Ps. 9:3–4).

- Believe God that the last deeds of our lives would be even greater than our earlier ones (Rev. 2:19).
- Believe God that with His strength we will miraculously finish strong and be able to say what our Lord stated at the end of His life: "I glorified You on the earth by accomplishing the work which You have given Me to do" (John 17:4).

We are not adequate for any of this, and that is why our precious Lord has given us the Holy Spirit to teach us and enable us to pray.

Join me in believing God in this closing prayer:

Lord, You tell us in Your Word that prayer can bring delight to Your heart (Prov. 15:8). May You teach each

*of us what You meant when You commanded us to pray
in the Holy Spirit so that great delight will come to Your
heart, and we will experience Your loving support to
fulfill Your eternal and wise purposes. For the glory of
Your name, we believe You to answer this request above
and beyond all we can ask or imagine! Amen.*

For Personal and Group Reflection

Look at the closing pages of this book and believe God for
the following blessings:

- Believe God to use our lives to love His world. He
  who sits on His throne, judging righteously, will
  maintain this just cause (1 Cor. 13:1–3).

  "When my enemies turn back, they stumble and
  perish before You. For You have maintained my
  just cause; You have sat on the throne judging
  righteously" (Ps. 9:3–4).

- Believe God that the last deeds of our lives would be even greater than our earlier ones (Rev. 2:19).
- Believe God that with His strength we will miraculously finish strong and be able to say what our Lord stated at the end of His life: "I glorified You on the earth by accomplishing the work which You have given Me to do" (John 17:4).

Acknowledgments

It is a pleasure to acknowledge my debt to the Lord Jesus Christ, who has graciously met me in my weakness and freed me from many misconceptions about prayer in order to teach me His refreshing truths. I am indebted to the loving and intimate prayer of my dear wife, Penny, and the companionship of my three sons, Will, Michael, David, and their precious families.

I am grateful to Paul Santhouse for his support in this project and for the capable team of Moody Publishers—Duane Sherman, who initiated this book, and Catherine Parks, Connor Sterchi, and Jacob Iverson—who followed through with it and made the idea of this book a reality. I would also acknowledge the capable editorial assistance of Amanda Cleary Eastep!

Almost fifty years ago I was led to give away my summer salary to support a very significant conference in

Korea—Explo '74. Little did I know that a young man and young woman who attended that conference would meet and marry and raise a godly son who would later come to Moody to study. That godly son—Sungbum Yi—has greatly aided me as my teaching assistant and so carefully typed the manuscript.

I am also grateful to the wonderful colleagues and so many precious students at the Moody Bible Institute who have enriched my life. Special thanks to former and present seminary school deans—B. Wayne Hopkins, Joe Henriques, John Jelinek, Winfred Neely—who have allowed me to teach a course on prayer at the Moody Theological Seminary for many years.

Notes

Preface

1. Sylvia Gunter, *For the Family* (Birmingham, AL: The Father's Business, 1994), 37. Used by permission: ©1994, For The Family by Sylvia Gunter, The Father's Business, P.O. Box 380333, Birmingham, AL 35238, www.thefathersbusiness .com.

Chapter 3

1. For more insight on what it means to delight in the Lord, see pages 62–66 in my book *Living the Life God has Planned—A Guide to Knowing God's Will* (Chicago: Moody, 2001).

Chapter 4

1. E. M. Bounds, *The Essentials of Prayer*, rev. ed. (Abbotsford, WI: Aneko Press, 2018), 13.

Chapter 5

1. Bill Thrasher, *A Journey to Victorious Praying: Finding Discipline and Delight in Your Prayer Life* (Chicago: Moody, 2017), 51.
2. Richard Foster, *Celebration of Discipline* (New York: Harper Collins, 1998), 35.
3. This was a statement that I heard from a message that J. Oswald Sanders gave at a chapel service at Moody Bible Institute.
4. Sammy Tippit, *The Prayer Factor* (Chicago: Moody, 1988), 87.

Chapter 6

1. C. S. Lewis, *Letters to Malcom: Chiefly on Prayer* (New York: Mariner Books, 2012), 82. A similar quote by C. S. Lewis is, "We must lay before Him what is in us, not what ought to be in us." Lewis, *Letters to Malcolm*, 22.

Chapter 8

1. For how to transform your anxiety into peace, see pages 185–194 of my book *A Journey to Victorious Praying: Finding Discipline and Delight in Your Prayer Life* (Chicago: Moody, 2017).
2. For an explanation of this truth, see pages 98–130 of my book *How to Be a Soul Physician* (Mexico: Berea Publishing Co., 2010), available at www.victoriouspraying.com.

3. For an explanation of this truth, see pages 132–55 of my book *How to Be a Soul Physician*.

Chapter 9

1. For further insights in experiencing God's cleansing, see pages 208–34 in my book *How to Be a Soul Physician* (Mexico: Berea Publishing Co., 2010), available at www .victoriouspraying.com.
2. These four questions are from an article that I read a number of years ago that was published by Life Action Ministries.
3. These are from J. Edwin Orr's video lecture on "The Role of Prayer in Spiritual Awakening," where he quotes these challenges by Evan Roberts.
4. These insights are taken from an article written by Bill Elliff that was sent from the OneCry ministry and emailed on September 19, 2019.
5. An unrepentant heart can abuse this truth, but a truly repentant heart needs it and finds great freedom in this truth. Never underestimate God's ability to take the mess you have made and overrule it for good.
6. The full story is in Genesis 20:1–18.

Chapter 10

1. J. C. Ryle, *Christian Leaders of the 19th Century* (Carlisle, PA: The Banner of Truth Trust, 1981), 83.

2. Bill Thrasher, *A Journey to Victorious Praying: Finding Discipline and Delight in Your Prayer Life* (Chicago: Moody, 2017), 60–61.

Chapter 12

1. The story of Katherine Rudy is from a typed document of several pages that Gil Beers gave me after speaking on "Heritage" to our father-son club. I was so impressed with this talk that I asked him for it in print and he kindly provided me with this printed copy. This is the source of the story I write at the end of this chapter.

Chapter 13

1. Ruth Graham Bell, *Prodigals and Those Who Love Them* (Colorado Springs: Focus on the Family, 1991), 69.

Chapter 14

1. Bill Thrasher, *A Journey to Victorious Praying: Finding Discipline and Delight in Your Prayer Life* (Chicago: Moody, 2017), 54–56.
2. Richard Harvey, *Seventy Years of Miracles* (Camp Hill, PA: Horizon House, 1998), 64–65.
3. Ibid., 66.
4. Ibid.

Christians often know the *theory* of the
Spirit-filled life but not the joy-filled *experience*.

More by Bill Thrasher...

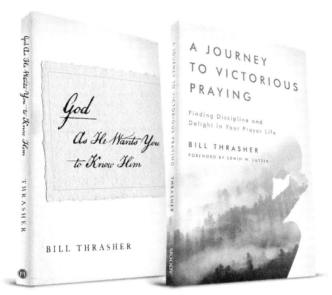

MOODY
Publishers®
From the Word to Life®

Bill Thrasher communicates essential theology with pastoral wisdom and compassion at an extremely approachable level in *God as He Wants You to Know Him*. For continued encouragement in your prayer life, read *A Journey to Victorious Praying*, where Thrasher addresses common misconceptions about prayer and offers practical, biblical truth.

978-0-8024-0422-0 | also available as an eBook | 978-0-8024-1563-9 | also available as an eBook and audiobook

Good things come to those who believe . . . right?

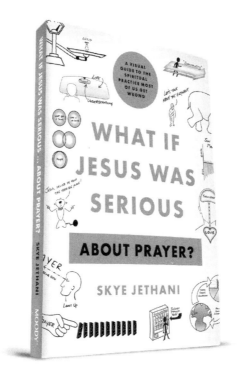